BLS WORKING PAPERS

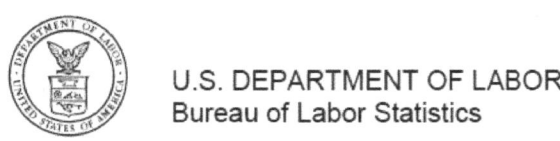 U.S. DEPARTMENT OF LABOR
Bureau of Labor Statistics

OFFICE OF PRICES AND LIVING
CONDITIONS

Incorporating Observed Choice into the Construction of
Welfare Measures from Random Utility Models

Roger H. von Haefen, U.S. Bureau of Labor Statistics

Working Paper 349
November 2001

I would I ke to thank my dissertation advisor, V. Kerry Smith, for many helpful comments and suggestions. Holger Sieg, Bill Desvousges, Randy Kramer, Dan Graham, and three anonymous referees were also instrumental in the development of this paper. Peter Feather and Daniel Hellerstein generously provided the data used in the empirical application. I take full respons bility for all remaining errors. The views expressed are those of the author and do not necessarily reflect the policies of the U.S. Bureau of Labor Statistics or the views of other staff members.

Incorporating Observed Choice into the Construction of Welfare Measures from Random Utility Models

Roger H. von Haefen[†]
Research Economist
Division of Price and Index Number Research
U.S. Bureau of Labor Statistics
Postal Square Building, Room 3105
2 Massachusetts Ave, NE
Washington, DC 20212-0001
Phone – (202) 691-6593
Fax – (202) 691-6583
von_Haefen_R@bls.gov

Final Version – September 6, 2001

[†] I would like to thank my dissertation advisor, V. Kerry Smith, for many helpful comments and suggestions. Holger Sieg, Bill Desvousges, Randy Kramer, Dan Graham, and three anonymous referees were also instrumental in the development of this paper. Peter Feather and Daniel Hellerstein generously provided the data used in the empirical application. I take full responsibility for all remaining errors, and all views expressed in this paper are mine alone and do not reflect the views or policies of the Bureau of Labor Statistics or its staff members.

Incorporating Observed Choice into the Construction of Welfare Measures from Random Utility Models

ABSTRACT

This paper develops an approach to welfare measurement from random utility models that incorporates the implications of an individual's observed choice. The economic and statistical properties of the proposed approach are discussed, and its empirical implications are illustrated with an application to outdoor recreation demand. Welfare estimates for two policy scenarios and four alternative repeated discrete choice specifications – a conditional logit, a quasi-nested logit, a random marginal utility of income logit, and a full random coefficients logit – are constructed for a subsample of the 1994 National Survey of Recreation and the Environment.

Key Words: Welfare Measurement, Random Utility Models, Simulation

1. INTRODUCTION

This paper develops an approach to welfare measurement from random utility models (RUMs) that conditions on an individual's observed choice. The economic and statistical properties of the proposed conditional approach to welfare measurement are compared with the unconditional approaches developed by Small and Rosen [35] and Hanemann [16], and a subsample of the 1994 National Survey of Recreation and the Environment (NSRE) is used to illustrate its empirical implications. Conditional and unconditional welfare estimates for two policy scenarios and four repeated discrete choice specifications (e.g., Caulkins [10], Morey, Rowe, and Watson [28]) are presented. These estimates suggest that: 1) sample means of conditional and unconditional welfare estimates are qualitatively similar but often diverge by more a correctly specified model would predict; 2) the conditional estimates appear to be more robust across alternative model specifications; and 3) the distribution of benefits implied by the conditional and unconditional estimates are qualitatively different.

The conditional approach to welfare measurement has some precedence in both the non-market valuation and marketing literatures. The notion that alternative interpretations of the factors that give rise to randomness in applied demand analysis imply different welfare estimators was first argued by Bockstael and Strand [6] in the context of single-equation demand models. Smith [36] later criticized their work because it failed to account for the fact that every demand model is in some sense misspecified. His criticism is particularly relevant in the context of RUMs because misspecification can cause sample means of conditional and unconditional consumer surplus estimates to diverge significantly. Similarly in the marketing literature, Allenby and Rossi [2] and Train and Revelt [43] have recently proposed estimating an individual's "partworth" (i.e., marginal utility) for a commodity characteristic by conditioning on her observed choice(s). These authors argue that a comparison of sample means of individual unconditional and conditional partworths can serve as an informal specification test. Both of these insights have close parallels with the conditional approach to welfare measurement developed in this paper.

The paper is organized as follows. Section 2 develops the theory of the conditional approach to welfare measurement and discusses its economic and statistical properties. Section 3 details the recreation data set used in the empirical analysis, and Section 4 reports parameter estimates from four repeated discrete choice specifications – a standard conditional logit, a quasi-nested logit proposed by Train [40] and Herriges and Phaneuf [18], a random marginal utility of income (RMUI) logit, and a full random coefficients logit model - used to model consumer choice. Section 5 then describes the two welfare scenarios considered, and Section 6 discusses the procedures used to construct unconditional and conditional Hicksian welfare estimates. Section 7 presents and interprets these estimates for the alternative policy scenarios and model specifications, and Section 8 concludes.

2. THEORY

This section discusses the theoretical foundations of the conditional approach to welfare measurement and its relationship to the unconditional approach developed by Small and Rosen [35] and Hanemann [16]. Although both approaches can be applied to all choice models employing the random utility hypothesis, this section uses the repeated discrete choice model of recreation demand (e.g., Caulkins [10], Morey, Rowe, and Watson [28]) to structure the discussion. In addition to simplifying exposition, focusing on this model is natural given the empirical application that follows.

The repeated discrete choice framework assumes that the individual's seasonal recreation demand arises from a series of discrete choices made on T separable choice occasions. On each choice occasion, the individual decides whether to take a single trip to one of J recreation sites or to stay at home (hereafter referred to as site 0).[1] The central building block for the model is the choice occasion conditional indirect utility function. Individual preferences on choice occasion t for the jth choice alternative ($j \in 0,...,J$) can be represented by the following conditional indirect utility function:

$$V((y_t - p_j)/p_z, \boldsymbol{q}_j, \varepsilon_{tj}) \qquad (1)$$

where y_t is the amount of seasonal income the individual allocates to choice occasion t, p_j is the individual's travel cost or price of visiting site j, p_z is the price index for the Hicksian composite commodity, and $\boldsymbol{q}_j$ is a vector of site specific characteristics such as environmental quality.[2] ε_{tj} summarizes additional factors specific to the individual, site j, and choice occasion t that are known by the individual but unobserved and random from the researcher's perspective. On each choice occasion, the rational individual will choose site k if:

$$V((y_t - p_k)/p_z, \boldsymbol{q}_k, \varepsilon_{tk}) \geq V((y_t - p_j)/p_z, \boldsymbol{q}_j, \varepsilon_{tj}), \quad j = 0, ..., J. \qquad (2)$$

Researchers are frequently interested in using the repeated discrete choice structure to estimate the seasonal Hicksian consumer surplus arising from changes in site characteristics such as environmental quality.[3] The conventional approach in the existing literature to constructing seasonal welfare measures from the repeated discrete choice framework involves two steps (e.g., Morey [27]). The researcher first constructs Hicksian consumer surplus estimates separately for each choice occasion conditional on the individual's fixed income allocation prior to the quality change.[4] Choice occasion welfare estimates are then summed across the T choice occasions to form an estimate of the individual's seasonal Hicksian consumer surplus.

Assuming $y_t = \bar{y}_t$, the Hicksian consumer surplus on choice occasion t, CS_t, associated with a change in q from $\boldsymbol{q}'$ to $\boldsymbol{q}''$ is implicitly defined as:

$$Max_{j \in 0, ,J}[V((\bar{y}_t - p_j)/p_z, \boldsymbol{q}'_j, \varepsilon_{tj})] = Max_{j \in 0, ,J}[V((\bar{y}_t - p_j - CS_t)/p_z, \boldsymbol{q}''_j, \varepsilon_{tj})]. \qquad (3)$$

Equation (3) suggests that CS_t is in general a function of the elements of the $(J+1) \times 1$ ε_t vector which are known only by the individual. From the researcher's perspective, CS_t is a random variable that cannot be determined precisely. In applied welfare analysis, the researcher often assumes a parent distribution from which each element of ε_t is drawn. This assumption, along with the specified structure of preferences and the observable site and individual specific characteristics, allows the researcher to construct a measure of the central tendency of the distribution of CS_t such as its mean.[5]

The unconditional and conditional approaches to welfare measurement employ alternative strategies for resolving the researcher's uncertainty about CS_t. Both approaches employ the same structure of preferences in (1)-(3), but the conditional approach employs additional information about ε_t implied by an individual's observed choice. In microeconomic applications, the researcher often observes whether and which of the J sites the individual visits on choice occasion t at current conditions. This observed choice, along with the inequalities in (2), implies restrictions on the support of the distribution of ε_t that can be used in the construction of consumer surplus estimates. The conditional approach to welfare measurement incorporates these additional restrictions while the unconditional approach does not.[6]

The conditional and unconditional approaches to welfare measurement can be rationalized by alternative interpretations of the factors that give rise to randomness in RUMs. As suggested by Hausman and Wise [17], one can interpret the elements of ε_t as arising from the "random firing of neurons" (p 407) or the individual's state of mind at a point in time. Under this interpretation, it is doubtful that the ephemeral factors that give rise to ε_t convey meaningful information about the individual's value for recreation sites and their characteristics. Therefore, the researcher favoring this view would likely prefer the traditional unconditional approach to welfare measurement. Alternatively, one can interpret the elements of ε_t as arising from important unobserved individual, commodity, and choice occasion specific characteristics that are not otherwise captured in the economic model and would likely persist if the choice occasion were repeated. If the researcher believes this interpretation, the conditional approach to welfare measurement would likely be preferred.

Although the two approaches are conceptually distinct and may imply substantially different welfare estimates for a given choice occasion, the law of iterated expectations and the law of large numbers imply that these differences diminish as the researcher aggregates across choice occasions and individuals to construct sample welfare estimates. Specifically, the law of iterated expectations implies the following relationship between the unconditional and conditional expectations:

$$E(CS_t) = \sum_j \pi_{tj} E(CS_t \mid j \text{ chosen}) \tag{4}$$

where π_{tj} is the probability that the individual will choose site j on choice occasion t given current conditions and $E(CS_t \mid j \text{ chosen})$ is the expected Hicksian consumer surplus conditional on site j being chosen at current conditions. Using (4), the difference between the conditional and unconditional expected Hicksian consumer surplus can be written:

$$E(CS_t \mid k \text{ chosen}) - E(CS_t) = \sum_j (1_{tj} - \pi_{tj}) E(CS_t \mid j \text{ chosen}) \tag{5}$$

where 1_{tj} is an indicator function equal to 1 if $j = k$ and 0 otherwise. Because consumer choice is random from the researcher's perspective, equation (5) implies that the difference between the unconditional and conditional estimates can be thought of as a random variable. If the researcher has correctly specified the data generating process for the observed recreation choices, the expectation of 1_{tj} is π_{tj} and, by implication, the expectation of (5) is zero. Assuming further that (5) has a finite variance, the law of large numbers implies that differences between sample means of unconditional and conditional welfare measures should diminish as the sample size grows.

A maintained assumption required for this convergence is that the researcher has correctly specified the data generating process for the sample's observed choices. As Smith [36] has noted, this is a strong if not implausible assumption in many applications.[7] Due to data and/or modeling limitations that are often beyond the researcher's control, applied recreation demand models may exclude or mismeasure important individual or site characteristics, misspecify the structure of consumer preferences and/or the sites that enter each individual's choice set, or misspecify the parent distribution for the unobserved determinants of choice. In these cases, differences between unconditional and conditional welfare measures may arise. An important practical question is how much these sources of misspecification compromise the integrity of the constructed welfare estimates. One approach to answering this question is to compare unconditional and conditional welfare estimates. If large differences are found, the researcher has evidence suggesting that significant model misspecification is present.

3. DATA

This section describes the recreation data from the 1994 National Survey of Recreation and the Environment (NSRE) used to empirically assess the proposed conditional approach to welfare measurement. A collaborative effort of several federal agencies, the 1994 NSRE consisted of two survey modules that attempted to determine the impact of the natural environment on current participation in water-based outdoor recreation. The Economic Research Service (ERS) at the Department of Agriculture developed a module that collected information on the recreational activities of 378 residents of the lower Susquehanna River basin.[8,9] The analysis reported here focuses on the 157 trip-taking residents of the region who took a combined 2,471 boating, fishing, swimming, and nature viewing trips to 219 lakes, rivers, and streams within 100 miles of their homes.[10]

Complete water quality data for all of these destinations as well as the large number of unvisited lakes, rivers, and streams that support outdoor recreation in the region were not available, so an aggregate/zonal approach to site definition was developed. In particular, the 219 destinations visited by the sample were aggregated separately by lakes and rivers/streams into geographic zones that corresponded to the Pennsylvania Department of Environmental Protection's delineation of the region into "sub-subbasin" watersheds (i.e., hydrological drainage regions) that range in size from roughly 100 to 500 square miles. Because the Susquehanna River serves as a boundary for many of these watersheds and represents a unique water resource in the region, visited destinations along the river were aggregated separately into 11 reaches. This site definition protocol implied that up to 89 recreation sites could enter an individual's choice set.[11,12]

PCMiler [1] was used to estimate round trip travel distances and times for every combination of the 157 recreators and 219 visited water bodies. Travel costs to each of the 219 visited water bodies were then estimated for each recreator-visited water body combination as the round trip travel distance valued at $0.30 per mile plus the round trip travel time valued at one-third the wage rate (Cesario [11], McConnell and Strand [23]).[13] When the individual's wage rate was not available in the NSRE survey, predicted wages were imputed using the individual's reported demographics and parameter estimates from wage regressions based on the 1994 March Supplement to the Current Population Survey (Smith, Desvousges, and McGivney [37]). These travel costs were then averaged at the watershed/river reach level to form estimates of each individual's travel costs to each of the 89 defined recreation sites that were not visited. For water bodies the individual visited, however, her estimated travel cost to the visited water body was used instead.

Frey et al. [14] report that a major source of water quality impairment in the lower Susquehanna River basin is agriculture and silviculture runoff. As a result, many receiving waters in the region are eutrophic, i.e., suffer from elevated nutrient levels that accelerate the naturally occurring photosynthetic process beyond a water body's assimilative capabilities. Algal blooms, ammonia odors, reduced water clarity, and impairments of flora and fauna life frequently result. All of these impacts would make a site less attractive to recreators and reduce their likelihood of visiting.

To represent these impacts at the 89 defined recreation sites, this analysis employs water quality index measures generated from multiple readings of water quality chemistries. Two index variables were constructed for all 89 sites. The first index variable, TSI, is constructed as a weighted average[14] of the following formulas that standardizes phosphorus and secchi disk readings into Carlson's [8] Trophic State Index:

$$TSI = 10 \times (6 - (48/Phos)/\ln(2)$$

$$TSI = 10 \times (6 - \ln(SD)/\ln(2)$$

where phosphorus (Phos) is measured in milligrams per liter (mg/l) and secchi disk (SD) is measured in meters. According to the EPA (Moore and Thornton [26]), TSI measures above 50 suggest that a receiving water is eutrophic. Given that small to moderate increases in phosphorus and other nutrient loadings at water bodies with low TSI levels might increase the amount of flora and fauna life to levels that may be preferable to recreators, all of the empirical specifications assume the TSI variable enters preferences in a quadratic form. A second water quality index, Lowdo, is a dummy variable that captures more advanced eutrophic conditions where surface water dissolved oxygen levels have fallen below safe levels for many fish species. According to the EPA (Novotny and Olem [30]), cold and warm water fisheries are impaired for fauna life when 30-day dissolved oxygen readings fall below 6.5 and 5.5 mg/l, respectively.

The raw water quality chemistry data that was used to construct the TSI and Lowdo indexes were collected from the EPA, the Pennsylvania Fish and Boat Commission, the Susquehanna River Basin Commission, and the Army Corps of Engineers. These water quality chemistries were first cleaned and then attached to each of the 219 visited water bodies using an iterative algorithm described in von Haefen [44]. The TSI and Lowdo indexes were then constructed for each visited water body. Similar to the construction of travel cost estimates for the 89 defined sites, these indexes were then averaged at the watershed/river reach level to form site specific indexes for all sites unvisited by each individual. For visited sites, the water quality indexes specific to the visited water bodies were used instead.

4. MODEL SPECIFICATION AND PARAMETER ESTIMATES

Four parametric specifications of the repeated discrete choice model are employed in the empirical application. For all four, the recreation season consists of 100 separable choice occasions,[15,16] the marginal utility of income is assumed to be constant on each choice occasion,[17] and the choice occasion conditional indirect utility functions are assumed to share a common linear-in-parameters and additive structure, i.e.:

$$V_{tj} = \lambda_t (y_t - p_j)/p_z + \beta_t q_j + \varepsilon_{tj}, \quad j = 0,...,J \tag{6}$$

where λ_t and β_t are estimable parameters. Table 1 defines the variables included in all specifications. The first specification considered is the standard conditional logit model (McFadden [24]). This specification arises if the researcher assumes that the ε_t elements are independent and identically distributed draws from the Type I Extreme Value distribution and the conditional indirect utility function's structural parameters are constant across individuals and choice occasions (i.e., $\lambda_t = \lambda$, $\beta_t = \beta$). A limitation with the conditional logit specification is that the ratios of the implied choice probabilities are independent of the composition of the choice set. This is the well-known independence of irrelevant alternatives restriction. The second specification generalizes the conditional logit specification by allowing the no trip dummy variable to vary randomly across individuals and choice occasions while holding the remaining parameters fixed. As Cardell [7], Train [40], and Herriges and Phaneuf [18] have argued, this random coefficients logit specification (McFadden and Train [25]) is conceptually similar to a nested logit model with all recreation sites aggregated into a single nest. In the remainder of the paper, the specification is referred to as a quasi-nested logit. It differs from a traditional nested logit only in the assumed distribution for the no trip dummy variable parameter, which in this application is normally distributed.[18]

A second random coefficients logit specification assumes that the marginal utility of income, λ_t, varies randomly across individuals and choice occasions with the remaining parameters (including the no trip dummy variable) fixed. For economic consistency, λ_t is assumed to be strictly positive and to follow a log-normal distribution. An appealing attribute of this random marginal utility of income (RMUI) specification is that differences in λ_t (and by implication the marginal rates of substitution between the Hicksian composite good and site quality) as well as ε_t across the season help to explain the individual's decision of when and where to recreate. The final specification considered assumes that all structural parameters vary randomly across individuals and choice occasions. This full random coefficients logit specification (Train [39]) assumes that on each choice occasion, each individual's vector of structural parameters can be treated as independent and identically distributed draws from a known distribution. For this application, the distributions employed are the log-normal distribution for λ_i and the normal distribution for the remaining parameters.

Given the closed form solutions for the choice probabilities, estimation of the conditional logit model is straightforward and accomplished with standard maximum likelihood techniques. For the quasi-nested logit, the RMUI, and the random coefficients logit specifications, however, the choice probabilities do not have closed form solutions. Since there is only one random coefficient in both the quasi-nested logit and the RMUI specifications, univariate numerical integration (i.e., Simpson's Rule) can be used to construct the likelihood function and recover structural parameter estimates within the maximum likelihood framework. Estimation of the full random coefficients logit specification, however, requires simulation based techniques (see Stern [38] for an overview). Given the relatively small recreation data set employed in this application (157 individuals) and the relatively large choice sets (up to 89 sites), estimating the model's structural parameters precisely was found to be computationally difficult using standard frequency simulator techniques as in Train [39]. To ameliorate this difficulty, a quasi-random simulator was employed. Following Bhat [5] and Train [41], Halton draws were used in place of random draws.[17] Experimentation based on increasing the number of Halton draws in 50 unit increments suggested that parameter estimates stablized when 500 or more draws were used. Therefore, the parameter estimates for the full random coefficients logit model reported in this paper were generated with 500 Halton draws.

Table 2 reports the parameter estimates and their asymptotic t-statistics for the four specifications. Beginning with the conditional logit specification, the estimates strongly suggest individuals prefer lower travel costs and sites with better environmental quality as measured by the Lowdo and TSI variables. The quadratic TSI specification suggests that TSI levels greater than 26 decrease consumer utility at an increasing rate. Individuals also prefer to visit sites along the Susquehanna River and located within federal, state, and county parks. Moreover, males and boaters, fishers, and swimmers are more likely to recreate. Parameter estimates for the quasi-nested logit specification are qualitatively similar to the conditional logit estimates, and the standard error parameter for the no trip dummy is highly significant. Once again, TSI levels greater than 26 decrease consumer utility at an increasing rate, and low dissolved oxygen levels negatively impact consumer utility.

The likelihood value for the RMUI specification suggests that allowing the travel cost coefficient to vary randomly across choice occasions and individuals results in a model that fits the data better than the conditional logit and the quasi-nested logit. The marginal utility of income is found to vary substantially across choice occasions but on average equals 2.371, and the water quality variables for this specification are qualitatively similar to the first two models (e.g., TSI levels greater than 27 decrease utility at an increasing rate). Finally, the parameter estimates for the random coefficients logit specification suggests that there is considerable heterogeneity across individuals and sites. For this specification, the expected marginal utility of income is estimated to be 2.959, low dissolved oxygen levels have significantly different impacts across individuals and choice occasions but in general decrease utility substantially, and TSI levels greater than 27 on average diminish the attractiveness of a recreation site at an increasing rate.

5. WELFARE SCENARIOS

In the recreation literature, two generic types of policy scenarios are often considered. One type evaluates the benefits arising from the improvement of water quality conditions in a watershed, river basin, or other large geographic region (e.g., Parsons and Kealy [31]), while a second considers the addition or loss of one or a small set of sites arising from more acute, geographically concentrated environmental impacts (Parsons, Plantinga, and Boyle [32]). This section uses policy scenarios from each of these broad categories to demonstrate and evaluate the conditional approach to welfare measurement.

The first scenario involves the cleanup of sites with low dissolved oxygen and high Trophic State Index (TSI) levels to safe standards as defined by the EPA. Welfare estimates from this scenario can inform policy makers of the potential benefits arising from the basin-wide cleanup of eutrophic sites. As noted earlier, the EPA defines warm and cold water bodies with dissolved oxygen levels greater than 5.5 and 6.5 mg/l, respectively, and TSI levels less than 50 as unimpaired. This policy therefore involves: 1) raising dissolved oxygen levels at impaired site such that the Lowdo variable equals zero at every site; and 2) lowering (raising) phosphorus levels (secchi disk readings) such that the TSI variable is less than 50 at every site. 70 of the 157 recreators in the sample took a combined 347 trips to at least one of the 22 eutrophic sites.

The second policy scenario considers the loss of a 40 mile reach of the lower Susquehanna River from Columbia, PA to Havre de Grace, MD. This reach corresponds to three of the 89 defined recreation sites and contains three state parks supporting a wide range of recreational opportunities such as boating, fishing, swimming, nature viewing, and hiking. 25 recreators in the sample took a total of 235 trips to the three sites that encompass the 40 mile stretch.

6. PROCEDURES FOR CONSTRUCTING HICKSIAN WELFARE MEASURES

This section outlines the procedures used to construct conditional Hicksian welfare measures for the four repeated discrete choice specifications. As noted in Section 2, the standard procedure for constructing an individual's seasonal willingness to pay from the repeated discrete choice framework involves first constructing Hicksian consumer surplus estimates separately for each choice occasion and then aggregating these estimates across choice occasions. Both unconditional and conditional welfare estimates reported in this paper employ this convention. Since constructing seasonal welfare measures is straightforward once choice occasion welfare measures have been generated, the discussion that follows focuses on Hicksian welfare estimation at the choice occasion. To highlight the differences between the conditional and unconditional approaches, the section begins with a discussion of how unconditional welfare estimates are constructed.

Given the structure of preferences in (6), the individual's Hicksian consumer surplus associated with a change in quality from q' to q'' on choice occasion t is:

$$CS_t = \frac{p_z}{\lambda_t}\left[Max_j\left[-\lambda_t p_j / p_z + \beta_t q''_j + \varepsilon_{tj}\right] - Max_j\left[-\lambda_t p_j / p_z + \beta_t q'_j + \varepsilon_{tj}\right]\right] \qquad (7)$$

The unconditional expectation of (7) is:

$$E(CS_t) = \int (CS_t) f(\lambda_t, \beta_t, \varepsilon_t) d\lambda_t d\beta_t d\varepsilon_t \qquad (8)$$

where $f(\lambda, \beta, \varepsilon_t)$ is the unconditional distribution of the structural parameters and ε_t. Given the assumed conditional independence of the structural parameters and ε_t, (8) can be rewritten as follows:

$$E(CS_t) = \int E(CS_t \mid \lambda, \beta_t) f(\lambda_t, \beta) d\lambda_t d\beta_t \qquad (9)$$

The assumption that each element of ε_t is an independent and identically distributed draw from the Type I Extreme Value distribution implies that $E(CS_t \mid \lambda, \beta_t)$ has a closed form solution, i.e.:

$$E(CS_t \mid \lambda_t, \beta_t) = \frac{p_z}{\lambda_t}\left[\ln\left[\sum_j \exp(-\lambda_t p_j / p_z + \beta_t q''_j)\right] - \ln\left[\sum_j \exp(-\lambda_t p_j / p_z + \beta_t q'_j)\right]\right] \qquad (10)$$

where the scale parameter for the Type I Extreme Value distribution has been normalized to one with no loss in generality. For the case where $\lambda_t = \lambda$ and $\beta_t = \beta$, (10) is the well-known "log-sum" formula (Small and Rosen [34], Hanemann [16]) that is used to construct unconditional welfare measures for the conditional logit specification.

For the more general specifications, (10) can also be used to generate estimates of $E(CS_t)$. Train [38] has proposed estimating $E(CS_t)$ for random coefficients logit models by using the following three step procedure: 1) simulate pseudo-random draws from the unconditional distribution of the structural parameters; 2) construct simulated estimates of (10) for each set of parameter draws; and 3) repeat steps

1) and 2) R times and average the simulated welfare estimates. For a sufficiently large R, this average will closely approximate $E(CS_t)$. This simulation algorithm is used for the full random coefficients model, and 2,500 random draws for each choice occasion were found to generate sample welfare estimates that changed by less than $0.10 with additional simulations. Similar to estimation, simulation is not required to construct estimates of $E(CS_t)$ for the quasi-nested logit model and RMUI logit specifications. Instead, one can use univariate numerical integration which is less computationally intensive.

Similar to equation (8), the conditional expectation of the Hicksian consumer surplus is:

$$E(CS_t \mid k \text{ chosen}) = \int (CS_t) f(\lambda_t, \beta_t, \varepsilon_{it} \mid k \text{ chosen}) d\lambda_t d\beta_t d\varepsilon_t \qquad (11)$$

where $f(\lambda_t, \beta_t, \varepsilon_t \mid k \text{ chosen})$ is the conditional distribution of the structural parameters and ε_t given the individual's observed choice of site k. For all four specifications, no closed form solutions for (11) exist in general, and simulation techniques are required. The simulation algorithm used here involves three steps: 1) simulate pseudo-random draws of λ_t, β_t, and ε_t from $f(\lambda_t, \beta_t, \varepsilon_t \mid k \text{ chosen})$; 2) For each set of simulated draws, use (7) to construct a simulated estimate of CS_t; and 3) repeat steps 1) and 2) R times and average the R simulated welfare estimates.

The practical difficulty with implementing this algorithm is generating simulated pseudo-random draws of λ_t, β_t, and ε_t consistent with the individual's observed choice. For this application, the strategy for accomplishing this task builds on the following decomposition of the joint distribution of λ_t, β_t, and ε_t conditional on the observed choice:

$$f(\lambda_t, \beta_t, \varepsilon_t \mid k \text{ chosen}) =$$
$$f(\lambda_t, \beta_t \mid k \text{ chosen}) f(\varepsilon_{tk} \mid \lambda_t, \beta_t, k \text{ chosen}) f(\varepsilon_t^{-k} \mid \varepsilon_{tk}, \lambda_t, \beta_t, k \text{ chosen}) \qquad (12)$$

where ε_t^{-k} is the ε_t vector without the kth component. (12) suggests that the researcher can simulate from $f(\lambda_t, \beta_t, \varepsilon_t \mid k \text{ chosen})$ by simulating first from $f(\lambda_t, \beta_t \mid k \text{ chosen})$ and then conditionally from $f(\varepsilon_{tk} \mid \lambda_t, \beta_t, k \text{ chosen})$ and $f(\varepsilon_t^{-k} \mid \varepsilon_{tk}, \lambda_t, \beta_t, k \text{ chosen})$. Of course, simulating from

$f(\lambda_t, \beta_t \mid k \text{ chosen})$ is trivial for the conditional logit specification. However, generating simulated

draws of λ_t and β_t is computationally difficult for all three random coefficients logit models. The

welfare estimates reported in this paper employ an adaptive Metropolis-Hastings simulator[20] described in

Sawtooth Software [33] and recently employed by Arora, Allenby, and Ginter [4]. The simulator falls

under the rubric of Markov Chain Monte Carlo (MCMC) simulators (Gelman et al. [15]) that are

frequently used in the Bayesian statistical literature to simulate from complex posterior distributions.

Appendix A describes the key steps of the simulator.

Conditional on a set of λ_t and β_t simulated draws, the researcher then simulates sequentially

from $f(\varepsilon_{tk} \mid \lambda_t, \beta_t, k \text{ chosen})$ and $f(\varepsilon_t^{-k} \mid \varepsilon_{tk}, \lambda_t, \beta_t, k \text{ chosen})$. Given the iid Type I Extreme Value

distribution for each element of ε_t, the marginal distribution for ε_{tk} and the conditional distribution for

each ε_{tj} $(j \neq k)$ are:

$$f(\varepsilon_{tk} \mid \lambda_t, \beta_t, k \text{ chosen}) = \exp(-\varepsilon_{tk})\exp((-1/\pi_{tk})\exp(-\varepsilon_{tk})) \tag{13}$$

$$f(\varepsilon_{tj} \mid \varepsilon_{tk}, \lambda_t, \beta_t, k \text{ chosen}) = \exp(\varepsilon_{tj})\exp(-\exp(-\varepsilon_{tj}) + \exp(-\varepsilon_{tk})(\pi_{tj}/\pi_{tk})), j \neq k \tag{14}$$

where π_{tj} and π_{tk} are the site choice probabilities conditional on the λ_t and β_t simulated draws.[21] The

researcher can simulate an ε_t vector consistent with the simulated structural parameters and the observed

choice by applying the probability integral transformation first to (13) and then to (14).

For the conditional logit specification where $\lambda_t = \lambda$, $\beta_t = \beta$, the researcher need only simulate

the ε_t vector using (13) and (14). For the policy scenarios considered in this paper, 2500 simulations

were found to generate seasonal welfare estimates that did not change by more than \$0.10 with additional

simulations. For the more general random coefficients logit specifications, the number of simulations

required to generate accurate estimates is substantially larger. As a result, 8000 simulations were used for

all three random coefficients logit specifications.[22]

7.   WELFARE ESTIMATES

Tables 3 and 4 report sample welfare statistics for both policy scenarios and all four specifications. Although unconditional and conditional estimates can be compared along several dimensions, the discussion here focuses on three: 1) a within-specification comparison; 2) an across-specification comparison; and 3) a comparison of distributional impacts.

Beginning with a pairwise comparison of unconditional and conditional sample mean welfare estimates for each policy scenario and specification, Table 3 suggests that the estimates are qualitatively similar and differ in absolute value by less than $5.00. Not surprisingly, these differences are largest for the conditional logit specification and considerably less for the more general random coefficients logit model. To help interpret whether the magnitude of these differences suggest that misspecification is present, a Monte Carlo experiment was developed. The experiment attempts to ascertain the magnitude of differences between the two estimates that should arise if the researcher has correctly specified the data generating process. Larger differences than what are predicted by the Monte Carlo experiment would suggest that misspecification is likely present. The technical details of the experiment are found in Appendix B, but its central finding is that one can expect differences of less than $1.00 for the cleanup of eutophic sites scenario and $2.00 for the loss of the lower Susquehanna River reach scenario from a correctly specified model. These findings suggest that some misspecification is likely present with the conditional logit, quasi-nested logit, and RMUI specifications, and that the differences arising from the random coefficients logit specification are consistent with a correctly specified model. An implication of these results is that the random coefficients logit model, which implies significantly larger welfare estimates compared to the other specifications in this application, may be the most credible specification for policy purposes.

Another dimension on which to compare the unconditional and conditional welfare estimates is their relative robustness across alternative model specifications. This dimension is important from a practical perspective because the researcher's choice of model specification is in some sense arbitrary and in all likelihood incorrect. For both scenarios, one finds that the conditional welfare estimates have a smaller range relative to the unconditional estimates ($18.62 versus $23.25 for the cleanup of eutrophic sites and $4.99 versus $9.63 for the loss of the lower Susquehanna River reach). Although these differences are small and should be interpreted cautiously, they suggest that conditional welfare measures may be less sensitive to the researcher's choice of model specification. Intuitively, this result may arise from the unconditional estimates' reliance on the estimated behavioral model for both predicting the recreator's trip choices at baseline conditions and structuring substitution among sites arising from the policy changes. The conditional welfare estimates, because they incorporate the recreator's observed choices at baseline conditions, use the behavior model only to structure substitution and thus are less model dependent. To the degree that baseline predictions are important determinants of Hicksian value, conditional estimates should be more robust across alternative model specifications. Thus, for example, one should expect relatively smaller differences in conditional welfare estimates for loss of site scenarios because the baseline number of trips to the lost site(s) - the critical determinant of Hicksian value with these scenarios - is held fixed at observed levels across specifications. The empirical results reported here support this interpretation, but further research is necessary before general conclusions can be drawn.

A third dimension on which to evaluate the conditional and unconditional welfare estimates is the implied distribution of impacts across the sample. Table 4 contains several sample statistics that help to elucidate the distributional implications of the unconditional and conditional estimates. For both policy scenarios and all four specifications, one finds average absolute differences between unconditional and conditional estimates for a given individual of roughly $20. For the cleanup of eutrophic sites scenario, the sample median, interquartile range, and minimum values are qualitatively similar between unconditional and conditional estimates, but the maximum conditional estimates are generally three to five times larger than the maximum unconditional estimates. This finding suggests that the conditional estimates imply a distribution of benefits that is more concentrated among a small subset of the sample. For the loss of the 40 mile reach of the lower Susquehanna River, this finding is more pronounced.

Although the unconditional estimates imply that roughly three-quarters of the sample suffer economic losses, the conditional estimates imply that less than one-quarter do. The latter finding is a reflection of the fact that only 22 of the 157 recreators in the sample (roughly 14 percent) visited one of the three sites that encompass the 40 mile reach. The conditional estimates imply that only these 22 recreators experience economic losses, whereas the unconditional estimates imply economic losses for a larger percentage of the sample.

8. CONCLUSION

This paper has proposed an approach to welfare measurement from random utility models that incorporates the implications of an individual's observed choice. The conditional approach to welfare measurement was motivated in the context of the repeated discrete choice model of recreation demand but is applicable to any choice model where the unobserved determinants of choice are given a behavioral interpretation. If the researcher has correctly specified the data generating process, the theory section suggested that differences between sample means of conditional and unconditional estimates diminish as the sample size increases. An empirical analysis based on a subsample of the 1994 NSRE found that differences between unconditional and conditional sample mean welfare estimates range from $0.93 to $4.49 in absolute value for two alternative policy scenarios and four model specifications. These differences were generally larger than what one would expect from a correctly specified model for all specifications except the full random coefficients logit model. Additionally, the results suggest that conditional welfare estimates may be more robust to alternative model specifications and imply a qualitatively different distribution of benefits. Although it is with considerable risk of error that one draws general implications from a single application, these results strongly suggest that the conditional approach to measurement has many interesting and desirable properties that warrant further investigation with alternative data sets and RUM-based structures.

9. SELECTED REFERENCES

1. Alk Associates, "PC Miler User Guide," Alk Associates, Princeton, NJ (1997).

2. G. Allenby and P. Rossi, Marketing Models of Consumer Heterogeneity, *J. Econometrics*, 89, 57-78 (1999).

3. American Chamber of Commerce, ACCRA Cost of Living Index: Comparative Data for 309 Urban Areas, 27(3), (1994).

4. N. Arora, G. Allenby, and J. Ginter, A Hierarchical Bayes Model of Primary and Secondary Demand, *Marketing Science*, 17, 29-44 (1998).

5. C. Bhat, Quasi-Random Maximum Simulated Likelihood Estimation of the Mixed Multinomial Logit Model, *Transportation Research,* Forthcoming.

6. N. Bockstael and I. Strand, The Effect of Common Sources of Regression Error on Benefit Estimates, *Land Econom.*, 10, 162-169 (1987).

7. N.S. Cardell, Variance Components Structures for the Extreme Value and Logistic Distributions with Application to Models of Heterogeneity, *Econometric Theory*, 13, 185-213 (1997).

8. R. Carlson, A Trophic State Index for Lakes, *Limnilogical Oceanography*, 22, 361-369 (1977).

9. R. Carson, W. M. Hanemann, and T. Wegge, "A Nested Logit Model of Recreation Demand in Alaska," Working Paper, University of California, San Diego (1989).

10. P. Caulkins, "An Empirical Study of the Recreational Benefits Generated by Water Quality Improvement," Ph.D. Dissertation, University of Wisconsin, Madison (1982).

11. F. Cesario, Value of Time in Recreation Benefit Studies, *Land Econom.*, 52, 32-41 (1976).

12. S. Chib and E. Greenberg, Understanding the Metropolis-Hastings Algorithm, *Amer. Statistician*, 49(4): 327-335 (1995).

13. W. Desvousges and S. Waters, "Report on Potential Economic Losses Associated With Recreation Services in the Upper Clark Fork River Basin, Volume III," Report submitted to the US District Court, District of Montana, in Relation to Pending Litigation between the State of Montana and the Atlantic Richfield Company (1995).

14. R. Frey et al., "Commonwealth of Pennsylvania 1996 Water Quality Assessment," Report Submitted in Compliance with Section 305(b), Federal Clean Water Act (1996).

15. A. Gelman et al., "Bayesian Data Analysis," Chapman & Hall: London, UK (1995).

16. W.M. Hanemann, Applied Welfare Analysis with Quantal Choice Models, Working Paper No. 173, Division of Agricultural Sciences, University of California, Berkeley (1981).

17. J. Hausman and D. Wise, A Conditional Probit Model for Qualitative Choice: Discrete Decisions Recognizing Interdependence and Heterogeneous Preferences, *Econometrica*, 46, 403-426 (1978).

18. J. Herriges and D. Phaneuf, Introducing Patterns of Correlation and Substitution in Repeated Logit Models of Recreation Demand, Working Paper, Department of Economics, Iowa State University (2001).

19. J. Huber and K. Train, On the Similarity of Classical and Bayesian Estimates of Individual Mean Partworths, *Marketing Letters*, 12, 257-267 (2001).

20. I. Krinsky and L. Robb, On Approximating the Statistical Properties of Elasticities, *Review of Economics and Statistics,* 68, 715-719 (1986).

21. I. Krinsky and L. Robb, On Approximating the Statistical Properties of Elasticities: A Correction, *Review of Economics and Statistics,* 72, 189-190 (1990).

22. K. Judd, "Numerical Methods in Economics," MIT Press, Cambridge, MA (1998).

23. K. McConnell and I. Strand, Measuring the Cost of Time in Recreation Demand Analysis: An Application to Sportfishing, *American Journal of Agricultural Economics*, 63, 153-56 (1981).

24. D. McFadden, Conditional Logit Analysis of Qualitative Choice Behavior, *in* "Frontiers in Econometrics," (Paul Zarembka, Ed.), Academic Press, New York, NY (1974).

25. D. McFadden and K. Train, Mixed MNL Models For Discrete Response, *J. Applied Econometrics*, 15, 447-470 (2000).

26. L. Moore and K. Thornton, Eds., "Lake & Reservoir Restoration Guidance Manual," Prepared by the North American Lake Management Society for the Environmental Protection Agency, Criteria and Standards Division, Nonpoint Source Branch, Report EPA 440/5-88-002 (1988).

27. E. Morey, TWO RUMS UNCLOAKED: A Nested Logit Model of Site Choice, and A Nested Logit Model of Participation and Site Choice, *in* "Valuing Recreation and the Environment," (C.L. Kling and J. Herriges, Eds.), Edward Elgar Publishing Ltd (1999).

28. E. Morey, R. Rowe, and M. Watson, A Repeated Nested-Logit Model of Atlantic Salmon Fishing, *Amer. J. Agri. Econom.*, 75, 578-592 (1993).

29. E. Morey and D. Waldman, Measurement Error in Recreation Demand Models: The Joint Estimation of Participation, Site Choice, and Site Characteristics, *J. Environ. Econom. Management*, 35, 262-276 (1998).

30. V. Novotny and H. Olem, "Water Quality: Prevention, Identification, and Management of Diffuse Pollution," Van Nostrand Reinhold, New York, NY (1994).

31. G. Parsons and M.J. Kealy, Randomly Drawn Opportunity Sets in a Random Utility Model of Lake Recreation, *Land Econom.*, 68, 93-106 (1992).

32. G. Parsons, A. Plantinga, and K. Boyle, Narrow Choice Sets in Random Utility Models of Recreation Demand, *Land Econom.*, 76, 86-99 (2000).

33. Sawtooth Software, The CBC/HB Module for Heirarchical Bayes Estimation, Technical Paper Available at Sawtooth Software's website, www.sawtoothsoftware.com/Techabs.htm (1999).

34. W.D. Shaw and P. Feather, Possibilities for Including the Opportunity Cost of Time in Recreation Demand Systems, *Land Econom.*, 75, 592-602 (1999).

35. K. Small and H. Rosen, Applied Welfare Economics with Discrete Choice Models, *Econometrica*, 49, 105-130 (1981).

36. V.K. Smith, Estimating Recreation Demand Using the Properties of the Implied Consumer Surplus, *Land Econom.*, 66, 111-120 (1990).

37. V.K. Smith, W. Desvousges, and M. McGivney, The Opportunity Cost of Travel Time in Recreation Demand Models, *Land Econom.*, 59, 259-278 (1983).

38. S. Stern, Simulation-Based Estimation, *J. Econom. Literature*, 35, 2006-2039 (1997).

39. K. Train, Recreation Demand Models with Taste Differences over People, *Land Econom.*, 74, 230-239 (1998).

40. K. Train, Mixed Logit Models for Recreation Demand, *in* "Valuing Recreation and the Environment," (C.L. Kling and J. Herriges, Eds.), Edward Elgar Publishing Ltd (1999).

41. K. Train, Halton Sequences for Mixed Logit, Working Paper, Department of Economics, University of California, Berkeley (1999).

42. K. Train, D. McFadden, and F.R. Johnson, Discussion of Morey and Waldman's 'Measurement Error in Recreation Demand Models,' *J. Environ. Econom. Management*, 40, 76-81 (2000).

43. K. Train and D. Revelt, "Customer-Specific Taste Parameters and Mixed Logit," Working Paper, Department of Economics, University of California, Berkeley (1999).

44. R. von Haefen, "Valuing Environmental Quality in a Repeated Discrete-Continuous Framework," Ph.D. Dissertation, Department of Economics, Duke University, Durham, NC (1999).

Appendix A

The Adaptive Metropolis-Hastings Simulation Algorithm

This appendix describes the adaptive Metropolis-Hastings algorithm that is used to simulate from $f(\lambda, \beta_t \mid k$ chosen$)$. This algorithm is similar to a set of procedures used by Sawtooth Software [33] to estimate Heirarchical Bayes discrete choice models. The algorithm involves the following steps:

1) At iteration r ($r = 1,\ldots,R$), a pseudo-random number generator is used to draw candidate structural parameters, $\tilde{\lambda}_t^r$ and $\tilde{\beta}_t^r$, separately for each individual/choice occasion combination. For $\tilde{\lambda}_t^r$, this is accomplished by simulating from the log-normal distribution with mean $\ln \tilde{\lambda}_t^{r-1}$ and standard error $d_r \sigma_{\ln \lambda}$, where d_r is a constant that is fixed across individuals and choice occasions and $\sigma_{\ln \lambda}$ is the standard error of $\ln \lambda_t$. Similarly, $\tilde{\beta}_t^r$ is generated from the normal distribution with mean vector $\tilde{\beta}_t^{r-1}$ and standard error vector $d_r \sigma_\beta$, where σ_β is the vector of standard errors of β_t. To initialize the sequence, $\tilde{\lambda}_t^0$ and $\tilde{\beta}_t^0$ are set equal to their unconditional expectations, i.e., $\tilde{\lambda}^0 = \exp(\mu_{\ln \lambda} + \sigma_{\ln \lambda}^2 / 2)$ and $\tilde{\beta}^0 = \mu_\beta$ where $\mu_{\ln \lambda}$ is the mean of $\ln \lambda_t$ and μ_β is the mean vector of β_t. The initial specification of d_r as well as its evolution across simulations is discussed in step 3) below.

2) For simulation r ($r = 1,\ldots,R$), calculate the following function separately for each choice occasion:

$$\psi_t^r = \frac{\pi_{tk}^r \times l(\tilde{\lambda}_t^r, \tilde{\beta}_t^r \mid \mu_\lambda, \sigma_\lambda, \mu_\beta, \sigma_\beta)}{\pi_{tk}^{r-1} \times l(\tilde{\lambda}_t^{r-1}, \beta_t^{r-1} \mid \mu_\lambda, \sigma_\lambda, \mu_\beta, \sigma_\beta)}$$

where π_{tk}^r is the predicted probability for individual i choosing site k (the site she is observed to choose) on choice occasion t conditional on $(\tilde{\lambda}_t^r, \tilde{\beta}_t^r)$ and $l(\tilde{\lambda}_t^r, \tilde{\beta}_t^r \mid \mu_\lambda, \sigma_\lambda, \mu_\beta, \sigma_\beta)$ is the likelihood function for $(\tilde{\lambda}_t^r, \tilde{\beta}_t^r)$. If $\psi_t^r \geq 1$, the researcher accepts the candidate structural parameter draws for the rth choice occasion (i.e., $\lambda_t = \tilde{\lambda}_t^r$ and $\beta_t = \tilde{\beta}_t^r$). If not, the researcher generates a random draw from the uniform distribution, say b_t^r, and accepts $\tilde{\lambda}_t^r$ and $\tilde{\beta}_t^r$ if $\psi_t^r \geq b_t^r$. If $\psi_t^r < b_t^r$, the reseracher rejects the candidate draws and accepts λ_t^{r-1} and β_t^{r-1} (i.e., $\tilde{\lambda}_t = \lambda_t^{r-1}$ and $\tilde{\beta}_t = \beta_t^{r-1}$).

3) For the rth simulation ($r = 1,\ldots,R$), estimate χ^r, the percentage of accepted candidate structural parameters for the sample. Call χ^r the jumping rule. Gelman et al. [15] state that the optimal jumping rule for the normal distribution is between 0.44 and 0.23 and decreases with the number of random coefficients. Following Sawtooth Software [33], the algorithm employed here targets the jumping rule to be around 0.30. To accomplish this, d_{r+1} is adjusted upwards (downwards) by ten percent if χ^r is greater (less) than .3. It is the continuous adjustment of d_{r+1} that makes this Metropolis-Hastings simulator *adaptive*. For $r = 1$, d_r is arbitrarily set to 0.1.

This Markov Chain Monte Carlo (MCMC) simulator was used to generate 9000 pseudo random draws of the structural parameters (i.e., $R = 9000$). As with any MCMC simulator, the sequence of draws can be regarded as a sample from the target density (in this case, $f(\lambda, \beta_t \mid k \text{ chosen})$) only after the chain has passed an initial stage and the effect of the arbitrarily specified starting values is minimal. Therefore, in this application, the initial 1000 simulations were dropped, and the remaining 8000 simulations were used to construct conditional welfare estimates.

Appendix B

Monte Carlo Experiment

This appendix discusses a Monte Carlo experiment that is used to generate benchmarks for evaluating whether differences between unconditional and conditional welfare estimates found with the NSRE data set suggest that model misspecfication is likely present. The experiment determines the magnitude of differences between the estimators the researcher should expect if she has correctly specified the data generating process. If the researcher finds differences greater than these benchmark values, she has evidence suggesting that some misspecification is present.

For computational ease, the Monte Carlo experiment employs the conditional logit specification and assumes that qualitatively similar results would arise from the more general random coefficients models. Assuming that the conditional logit specification with the parameter estimates reported in Table 2 is the true data generating process, simulated choices were generated for every individual and choice occasion in the NSRE recreation data set. This was accomplished by using the logit probabilities of site selection and a pseudo-random number generator. These simulated choices were used to estimate the structural parameters with standard maximum likelihood techniques. The structural parameter estimates and the simulated choices were then used to construct the sample means of unconditional and conditional welfare measures for the two policy scenarios. The absolute differences between the sample means of the unconditional and conditional welfare measures were constructed and saved in a separate data file.[23] This procedure was replicated 100 times and a box-and-whisker plot of the results is found in Figure 1.

Figure 1 suggests that the mean differences between the unconditional and conditional welfare measures are roughly $0.50 for both policies.[24] The interquartile ranges fall between $0.25 and $0.90 and are tighter for the cleanup of eutrophic sites scenario (policy 1). Although there are slightly more outliers for the loss of the lower Susquehanna River reach scenario (policy 2), the results generally suggest that differences between the unconditional and conditional approaches should be less than $1.00 and $2.00 for policies 1 and 2, respectively, if the researcher has correctly specified the data generating process.

Table 1
Variable Definitions

Tcost	Round trip travel cost estimates for each site entering each individual's choice set. Each travel cost is normalized by a 1994 regional price index generated by the American Chamber of Commerce [3].
Lowdo	Percentage of visited water bodies in the watershed/river reach with dissolved oxygen levels below 5.5 and 6.5 mg/l for warm and cold water bodies, respectively.
TSI	Average of Trophic State Index levels for visited water resources in the watershed/river reach. These indexes were constructed from phosphorus and secchi disk water quality chemistry data.
No Trip Dummy	= 1 for the no trip choice alternative, 0 otherwise.
Water × No Trip Dummy Interaction	= 1 for the no trip choice alternative if the individual participated in boating, fishing, or swimming outdoor recreation during the past year, 0 otherwise.
Female × No Trip Dummy Interaction	= 1 for the no trip choice alternative if the individual is female, 0 otherwise.
Susq	= 1 if recreation site is located along the Susquehanna River.
Park	Percentage of visited recreation water bodies located within a federal, state, or county park.

Table 2
Parameter Estimates for Alternative Repeated Discrete Choice Specifications

	Conditional Logit	Quasi-Nested Logit		Random Marginal Utility of Income (RMUI) Logit		Random Coefficients Logit	
		Mean	Standard Error	Mean	Standard Error	Mean	Standard Error
Log-Likelihood	-11,331.07	-11,295.91		-10,891.51		-10,260.17	
Tcost	-0.119[2]	-0.118	-	0.044	1.280	-0.049	1.506
	(-60.58)	(-58.12)		(0.266)	(14.36)	(-0.749)	(33.60)
Lowdo	-2.108	-2.117	-	-1.954	-	-19.05	10.27
	(-10.94)	(-10.82)		(-10.50)		(-7.205)	(8.316)
TSI/10	0.942	0.952	-	1.056	-	2.295	0.054
	(16.48)	(15.19)		(16.43)		(24.72)	(1.65)
$TSI^2/100$	-0.180	-0.183	-	-0.190	-	-0.411	0.013
	(-15.80)	(-14.69)		(-15.15)		(-22.98)	(2.192)
Susq	0.580	0.569	-	0.667	-	-34.20	30.41
	(9.770)	(8.812)		(9.971)		(-10.56)	(12.35)
Park	0.611	0.694	-	0.892	-	1.051	0.025
	(10.04)	(10.66)		(12.13)		(11.56)	(0.108)
No Trip Dummy	2.512	4.027	2.761	-0.044	-	-1.813	0.045
	(27.62)	(12.93)	(8.082)	(0.874)		(-7.140)	(0.171)
Water × No Trip Dummy	-0.150	-0.155	-	-0.007	-	4.080	6.249
	(-1.946)	(-1.144)		(0.067)		(8.358)	(11.63)
Female × No Trip Dummy	0.640	1.098	-	1.030		3.872	0.398
	(12.75)	(8.823)		(9.515)		(13.18)	(1.106)

[1] For the RMUI and random coefficients specification, Tcost is assumed to follow a log-normal distribution. The mean and standard error estimates for Tcost imply that the expected marginal utility of income (i.e., the negative of the expected marginal disutility of travel cost) is 2.371 and 2.959, respectively.

[2] Asymptotic t-statistics are reported in parentheses.

Table 3
Sample Welfare Estimates (1994 Dollars)[1]

	Conditional Logit	Quasi-Nested Logit	RMUI Logit	Random Coefficients Logit
Cleanup of Eutrophic Sites				
Unconditional Sample Mean	$23.44 (1.07)[2]	$23.48 (1.18)	$25.86 (1.53)	$46.69 (2.86)
Conditional Sample Mean	$27.93 (1.81)	$27.14 (1.53)	$28.53 (2.09)	$45.76 (1.85)
Difference	$4.49	$3.66	$2.67	-$0.93
% Difference	19.2	15.6	10.3	-2.0
Loss of 40 Mile Reach of lower Susquehanna River				
Unconditional Sample Mean	-$12.37 (0.49)	-$15.80 (0.77)	-$16.03 (0.95)	-$22.00 (0.81)
Conditional Sample Mean	-$15.46 (0.25)	-$16.75 (0.41)	-$18.08 (0.46)	-$20.45 (0.62)
Difference	-$3.09	-$0.95	-$2.05	-$1.55
% Difference	25.0	6.0	12.8	-7.0

[1] All welfare estimates constructed with sampling weights implied by county-stratified sampling design.

[2] Krinsky and Robb [20, 21] standard errors in parentheses. All unconditional standard errors were constructed with 200 simulations, whereas all conditional standard errors were constructed with 50 simulations.

Table 4
Sample Descriptive Statistics of the Unconditional and Conditional Welfare Estimates[1]

	Conditional Logit	Quasi-Nested Logit	RMUI Logit	Random Coefficients Logit
Cleanup of Eutrophic Sites				
Mean Absolute Difference Between Uncond./Cond. Estimates (per Recreator)[2]	$17.82	$19.70	$24.99	$23.32
Unconditional Estimates				
Median	$21.80	$21.06	$25.21	$38.16
Interquartile Range	[$9.60, $36.22]	[$11.59, $32.71]	[$14.72, $33.61]	[16.49, $70.53]
Minimum	$0.37	$0.39	$4.00	-$2.49
Maximum	$67.16	$78.67	$68.74	$160.11
Conditional Estimates				
Median	$19.85	$16.53	$12.51	$23.31
Interquartile Range	[$6.19, $35.87]	[$4.95, $30.94]	[$4.74, $31.48]	[$7.59, $52.14]
Minimum	$0.10	$0.03	$0.18	-$280.48
Maximum	$325.38	$328.85	$270.72	$448.94
Loss of 40 Mile Reach of lower Susquehanna River				
Mean Absolute Difference Between Uncond./Cond. Estimates (per Recreator)	$17.38	$19.72	$21.89	$25.49
Unconditional Estimates				
Median	$-2.29	-$2.66	-$6.14	-$5.40
Interquartile Range	[-$17.08, -$0.07]	[-$21.68, -$0.11]	[-$20.95, -$2.00]	[-$22.94, -$1.73]
Minimum	-$101.86	-$139.67	-$126.62	-$146.36
Maximum	$0.00	$0.00	$0.00	$0.00
Conditional Estimates				
Median	$0.00	$0.00	$0.00	$0.00
Interquartile Range	[$0.00, $0.00]	[$0.00, $0.00]	[$0.00, $0.00]	[$0.00, $0.00]
Minimum	-$415.11	-$428.88	-$422.32	-$345.70
Maximum	$0.00	$0.00	$0.00	$0.00

[1] All estimates constructed with sampling weights implied by the county-stratified sampling design.
[2] This statistic was constructed by first taking the difference between her expected unconditional and conditional welfare measures for each recreator. The absolute value of this difference was then constructed and averaged across the sample.

31

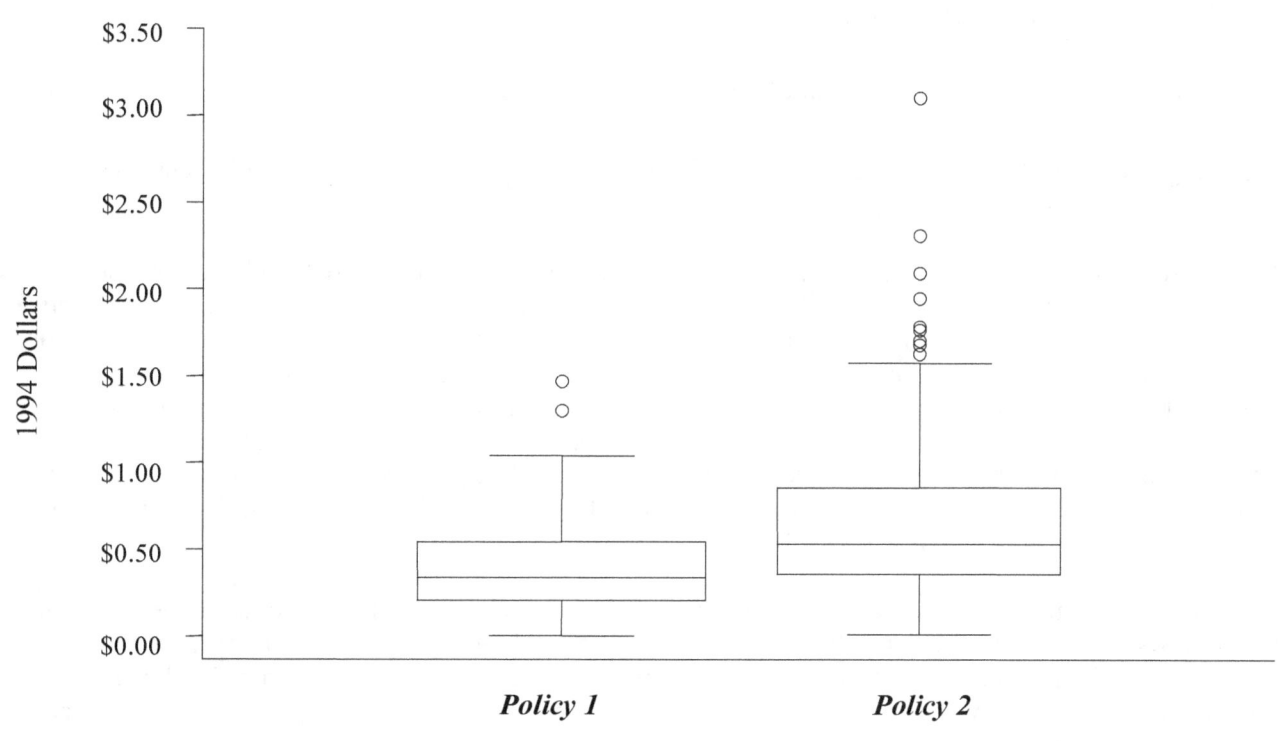

Figure 1
Box-and-Whisker Plot Graph of Absolute Differences between
Unconditional & Conditional Welfare Measures

Each box-and-whisker plot was generated with 100 simulations. The line inside each "box" represents the median of the empirical distribution. The interquartile range is contained inside each "box." The upper (lower) whisker represents the largest data points less than (greater than) or equal to the 75th (25th) percentile plus (minus) the interquartile range multiplied by 1.5. All data points outside this expanded range are plotted individually.

Footnotes

[1] Carson, Wegge, and Hanemann [9] and Desvousges and Waters [13] have proposed repeated discrete choice models where the choice occasion corresponds to a week and the individual may choose to take one or more trips to selected sites per week.

[2] It is assumed that p_{ij} and each element of q_j are equal to 0 for $j = 0$.

[3] Although not considered in the theory section, this discussion can be extended to valuing changes in site access such as the loss of a site.

[4] The assumption that the individual's income allocation is unaltered by the quality change is restrictive. In general, individuals will want to reallocate their seasonal income across choice occasions to maximize seasonal utility with a change in site quality. Restricting them to the income allocation they choose prior to the quality change implies that they will likely not achieve as high a level of seasonal utility as they would otherwise. As a result, seasonal welfare measures constructed using this two step procedure are biased downward to the degree that individuals want to reallocate their seasonal income. A special case where no bias is present arises when the researcher restrictively assumes a constant marginal utility of income on each choice occasion. This assumption is frequently used in applications of the repeated discrete choice model (e.g., Caulkins [10]).

[5] Hanemann [16] also considers other summary measures such as the median and mode. In the discussion that follows, these alternative summary measures are not considered because of the recreation literature's exclusive focus on the mean. This narrow focus, however, should not be interpreted as implying that the conditional approach to welfare measurement does not apply if the researcher prefers these alternative summary measures.

[6] It should be emphasized that the conditional approach to welfare measurement incorporates the same restrictions on ε_t that are used to derive the likelihood (i.e., the probability) of observing a given choice (see, e.g., Morey [27] for a formal derivation of the likelihood function). Since classical and Bayesian inference procedures employ the likelihood function, the conditional approach to welfare measurement is consistent with either approach to statistical inference. See Huber and Train [19] for a discussion of the similarities and differences of classical and Bayesian approaches to statistical inference with discrete choice models.

[7] Train, McFadden, and Johnson's [42] recent critique of Morey and Waldman's [29] proposed approach to accounting for measurement error in fish catch rates suggests that environmental economists are becoming increasingly sensitive to the implications of misspecification for welfare measurement.

[8] A second module, conducted by the EPA, surveyed residents from all 50 states, but only information on each individual's most recent boating, fishing, and swimming trips was collected.

[9] The ERS module also collected recreation data from residents of three other river basins – the Mid-Columbia in Washington state, the Central Nebraska, and the White River basin in Indiana. Because the amount of water quality chemistry data in the lower Susquehanna River basin was far more extensive relative to the other regions, the empirical analysis focuses exclusively on the lower Susquehanna.

[10] The ERS survey did not identify whether these trips were single day or multiple day trips, but because all trips are to local sites, they are treated as single day trips.

[11] To account for the fact that the NSRE survey collected data only on trips to local sites, only those sites located within 100 miles of each respondent's home were included in her choice set.

[12] von Haefen [44] finds qualitatively similar per trip welfare estimates for water quality improvements from the watershed-based 89 site model with the disaggregate 219 site model. Although the relationship between these two models and the "true" site definition model is unknown, these similar empirical findings suggest that the watershed-based approach to site definition might be a plausible way to define zonal sites.

[13] Although using one-third the wage rate for the opportunity cost of time is a widely used convention in empirical practice, its theoretical defensibility has been called into question with increasing regularity. See Shaw and Feather [34] for a recent discussion of the proper value of the opportunity cost of time in recreation demand models.

[14] The weights used were proportional to the amount of phosphorus and secchi disk data available at each site.

[15] As correctly noted by a referee, specifying the number of choice occasions requires a judgement by the researcher that is often arbitrary and lacking theoretical or intuitive appeal. Some additional results not reported in this paper that are based on models assuming 200 and 500 choice occasions, however, suggest that the specification of the number of choice occasions does not affect welfare estimates qualitatively in this application.

[16] Only three individuals in the sample reported taking more than 100 trips. The trip demands for these individuals were reduced proportionately across sites until their adjusted total trips equaled 100.

[17] This assumption implies that the individual's choice occasion income does not influence the recreation decision.

[18] Several additional multi-level quasi-nested logit specifications were also estimated, but the standard error parameter estimates for these more complicated models were not found to be statistically significant and are consequently not reported.

[19] Both Bhat [5] and Train [41] give intuitive descriptions of Halton draws and their relationship to random draws. Chapter 9 in Judd [22] gives a more general discussion of quasi-simulation procedures.

[20] See Chib and Greenberg [12] for a general discussion of the Metropolis-Hastings simulation algorithm.

[21] Because the scale parameter for the Type I Extreme Value distribution is not identified within the logit framework, equations (13) and (14) assume that it has been normalized to one.

[22] Using *GAUSS 3.5* and an 866 Mhz Pentium III processor with 256 Mb RAM, the full simulation algorithm for each of the random coefficients logit models took about 90 minutes.

[23] 2500 simulations were used to construct the conditional welfare estimates.

[24] For the 100 simulations, the mean absolute differences between the unconditional and conditional welfare measures are $0.40 and $0.69 for the cleanup of eutropic sites and the loss of the Susquehanna River reach, respectively. The median absolute differences are $0.34 and $0.53, respectively.